# Melissa's Game

Paul Davenport



Cornelsen

**Cornelsen English Library**
Paul Davenport

**Verlagsredaktion**
Martin Walsh

**Umschlaggestaltung**
Heike Börner

**Titelbilder**
Shutterstock
Sam Chadwick, Mandy Godbehear (oben)

**Illustration**
Constanze Schargan
Massachusetts Bay Transportation Authority (Subway map)

**Typografie**
Anna Bakalović und Annika Preyhs

**Technische Umsetzung**
Ilona und Ingo Ostermaier

**www.cornelsen.de**

1. Auflage, 1. Druck 2008

Alle Drucke dieser Auflage sind inhaltlich unverändert und können im Unterricht nebeneinander verwendet werden.



Druck: CS-Druck CornelsenStürtz, Berlin

ISBN 978-3-06-032123-0

Inhalt gedruckt auf säurefreiem Papier aus nachhaltiger Forstwirtschaft.

## Contents

## **Chapter 1** What a Feeling!

I felt so happy that I almost started singing out loud. Instead, I sang the song *What a Feeling* to myself, only moving my lips. It was the first day of my summer vacation and I was on the bus on my way to my favorite aunt who lived in Boston!

What a feeling! Aunt Deborah had invited me to stay at her place for a whole month! She said that the girl who lived next door, Melissa, couldn't wait to meet me. I was looking forward to meeting her, too. Melissa, she added, was an only child and both of her parents were doctors.

Within a few minutes of my arrival at my aunt's, Melissa came over and introduced herself. I liked her right from the start. We fitted together very well, I thought. She was my age, 16, and seemed very sure of herself. And me? Well, I was happy to let others take the lead. So, when Melissa said she knew Boston well and would love to show me around, I was delighted. "We'll have lots of fun, Dee," she said with a warm smile. "You'll see."

I had been to Boston a few times with my mother and thought I knew the place, but the Boston Melissa was talking about was more than just the downtown area I knew. She talked about Back Bay, with its trendy shops and restaurants, Fenway, where the Boston Red Sox play, Cambridge, home of Harvard University, Suffolk Downs, where the famous horse races take place and Revere Beach. To get there, all you have to do, she said, was jump on the subway. "The Big T", as it's called, will take you to any of these places and many more. It's the oldest subway in America and some people say "The Big T" is loud and bumpy; Melissa says it's cheap and gets you where you want to go fast.

The day after I arrived, it turned very warm and Melissa decided that the best place to go was Revere Beach. And she was right! With its long, sandy beach and cool breeze from the Atlantic, it was a great place to hang out. The water was clean, too, with no algae or jellyfish!

Not that we were in the water that much. We were beach potatoes. We spent most of our time on the beach checking out the boys. I was surprised. Boston boys seemed to be different than the boys from my hometown of Hartsville. Don't get me wrong. Hartsville boys are okay, they're just – well, a little boring. I don't blame them. They can't help it. It probably has to do with the fact that they grow up in Hartsville. The problem is, there's not that much going on for young people there. And everyone in Hartsville knows everyone else. Which is okay in a way, but not okay in many other ways. It's like everyone knows what you're doing most of the time. It's hard to have a private life, if you know what I mean.

But, as I said before, Boston boys seemed somehow different to me, and with Melissa at my side, it wasn't long before I got the chance to find out just how different they were.

## Chapter 2 Revere Beach

It was our second day there. We had been at the beach about an hour when along came this good looking dude, walking along the beach with his dog. Actually, dogs aren't allowed on the beach, but he didn't seem to know or care about that.

Anyway, his dog came over to us. (With a little help from Melissa, who called it and held out a piece of her sandwich.) And then, of course, he – the dude – came over, too.

Melissa broke the ice by raving about the dog. Its name was Norah, and it – she – was oh-so-cute. His name was Billy. He seemed a little nervous at first but talking about his dog loosened him up. After a while, we were all talking and laughing at the same time. Then Melissa had a great idea. Why don't we go down to Kelly's for one of their famous roast beef sandwiches? Billy wanted to, you could tell, but he didn't have any money with him. No problem, Melissa said. (She always had lots of money with her.)

So we all went to Kelly's – Billy, Norah, Melissa and me. It was a half-hour walk down the beach and we talked all the way.

I noticed the looks we were getting from the girls on the beach. Of course, they were looking more at Billy than at Melissa or me but still, it made me feel good.

Billy answered all of Melissa's questions. She asked him hundreds of questions. (She is very interested in people – especially boys.) He's in his second year at Revere High School. He doesn't do too well in his subjects, but he does like acting. He's in the drama club and is going to play the leading role in this year's play. His father is a captain in the navy. His mother, a former professional golf player, gives golf lessons. His little sister is in the seventh grade and is a much better student than him, etc., etc.

He told us all about Revere Beach. About its glorious past. Many years ago, it was *the* place to go in Boston, he said, especially for working class people. Besides the huge beach, there had been an amusement park, America's largest, which opened in 1906. It was the Disneyland of its time, with many spectacular attractions, including a Wild West Show with over 100 cowboys and – the most spectacular attraction of all – the awesome Cyclone, at that time the largest roller coaster in the United States. There were also roller skating rinks, bowling alleys and ballrooms, where the most famous bands of the day played, like the Tommy Dorsey Orchestra and Guy Lombardo and the Royal Canadians.

I asked him where all these things had gone and he said that there had been a terrible blizzard in the winter of 1958 which destroyed most of the buildings along the beach. But, he was quick to add, the city of Boston decided to restore the beachfront and after over ten years of reconstruction work, Revere Beach was officially reopened in 1992. I could see that Billy was proud of "his" beach and its history.

After eating at Kelly's (fantastic!) we walked on another half hour to Billy's place. He lived in Wonderland, not far from the beach. He invited us in and showed us around. Then he called Miles, his best friend. And that's when the fun really began.

- to show sb. around - jemanden herumführen
- to invite sb. in - jemanden einladen

## Chapter 3 Beach Flirt

The moment I saw Miles I liked him. He wore glasses and looked very serious, but you were in for surprise when you got to know him. He turned out to be a fun-and-action kind of guy. We were sitting around in Billy's room talking and listening to music when Miles suddenly said, "Hey let's go down to the beach and throw a Frisbee."

I said I'd never thrown one before, but Miles said he would help me learn how. It was a good thing that Billy had two Frisbees. That way, Billy and Melissa could throw to each other while I had my "lesson" with Miles.

He got up real close to show me the different grips and throwing techniques. He put his hand on mine and it felt nice and warm. I was a slow learner.

Finally, when the lesson was over, we joined the other two. It was amazing how far Miles could throw a Frisbee. Billy was good at it, too. Melissa and I were, well, beginners. We couldn't throw far but at least the Frisbee flew in the right direction – most of the time.

About an hour later, Miles suddenly stopped and said it was time for a milkshake. He pointed toward a little place down the beach and said they had Boston's best ice cream and milkshakes. I was going to say that I was on a diet but shut my mouth when I realized it wasn't the right moment to say something like that.

We got our milkshakes and went across the street to the long low wall that runs along the promenade. There we sat and watched the action on the beach. We drank our milkshakes (mine was coffee-flavored and the best I'd ever had!) and talked and laughed for what seemed like hours.

The sun was setting when Billy and Miles walked us to the subway station. They both said what a great time they'd had with us. They asked if we were coming back the next day. Melissa hesitated a moment, then said yes.

And we did. The next day and the next and the next. Altogether, our little "beach flirt" lasted a little more than a week. Until the day we didn't show up.

I was surprised when Melissa said we were going to another beach that day. We'd go to Constitution Beach, she said, in Orient Heights, on the same line but three stations before Revere Beach. When I asked her why the sudden change of plans, she only said it was time for something new.

I was disappointed. I would miss Miles. When Melissa saw my sad face she said that I was being silly. Summertime, she said, was a time for flirting and – there were lots more boys in Boston to flirt with.

That same day we met two more.

# Chapter 4 Michael and Ben

How did we meet them? That's a good question. Meeting boys is not that easy. It has to look – how can I put it? – natural. That's it. As if it wasn't intended, as if it just somehow happened. Melissa is an expert in that department.

We were lying on the beach "reading" when she noticed two boys walking by on their way to the water. She called out to them, could they tell us what time it was? They came over at once. Wow! I thought, and couldn't take my eyes off the taller boy. She got them talking and then asked them to tell us how cold the water was when they came back from swimming. Not very original, you might say. But Melissa is a good actress. She made it all look very – natural.

And it worked. When they came back a little later they hurried over to us and told us (what we already knew) that the water was a little on the cold side, but just warm enough for a quick swim. Melissa, of course, was ready with her next question. Had they seen any jellyfish? She was very afraid of jellyfish, she said.

By the time they had answered that and several more questions, one of them finally noticed the magazine Melissa had put beside her in the sand. His eyes almost popped out of his head. "Boston's Big Hitter?" he said. "Hey. It's an article about David Ortiz. You're into the Red Sox?" he said, looking at Melissa.

Yeah, Melissa was into the Red Sox, and she knew exactly how important that was for making contact with boys. There followed a long discussion about this year's team, the new players, the team's chances of winning the pennant, etc. I was amazed at how well informed Melissa was. I tried to look as interested as I could to cover up the fact that I knew little or nothing about what they were talking about. I told myself that I would have to follow the Red Sox more closely in the future.

After that, they asked if we'd like to join them for a coffee. Moments later, we were sitting outside a café laughing so loud that everyone was looking at us. Later, when we calmed down, Melissa got someone to take a photo of us. My smile for the camera came easily. Michael, the taller of the two, had put his arm on my shoulder! Ben, the other boy, got up real close to Melissa.

After that, we took a long walk down the beach. At first, we were together but after a while Ben and Melissa got ahead of us because Michael kept stopping to show me things on the beach. He knew all about the different kinds of shells and it was very interesting to listen to him talk about them. Then, after telling me about himself for a while, he wanted to know all about me. He asked very interesting questions and was such a good listener that I had the feeling I was saying these things for the first time.

That was the beginning of a beautiful friendship, but one that ended much too soon. After about a week, Melissa said she'd had enough of Constitution Beach and that it was time to show me around downtown Boston. I couldn't believe how cool Melissa was about it. It left me feeling very disappointed – again.

I felt angry and hurt and wanted to protest. Instead, I only nodded and forced a little smile.

# Chapter 5 Wanted Dead or Alive: Boys!

Late in the afternoon of the next day we took the Orange Line subway from Stony Brook, where she and my aunt live, to Downtown Crossing, the subway station in the heart of downtown Boston.

That's where our shopping tour began. For the next few hours we went up and down Washington Street looking for our kind of clothes. Melissa knew all the right places. She avoided the huge department stores like Macy's and Filene's and concentrated on the boutiques. I didn't buy that much, but Melissa was carrying two large shopping bags when we finished. When she asked me if I was ready to eat, I said yes immediately.

We hurried through the crowded streets and came to a large brick building in the middle of a square. This, she told me, is Faneuil Hall. I'd heard of it, I said and thought: it sure looks boring. Okay, there were a few nice restaurants on the outside but I wasn't really impressed – until we went inside and I saw and smelled the food! There were eateries all along both walls with every kind of food you could imagine: Mexican, Italian, Indian, Thai, Chinese, Japanese, Greek, … As we walked through the crowded passage, my eyes ran back and forth between the eateries, and in the end I just stood there, not knowing what to choose. Then I saw what Melissa was having: clam chowder and a lobster sandwich, Boston specialties, and I ordered the same.

As soon as we got our food, Melissa signaled for me to follow her. We soon came to a huge hall in the middle of the building with long wooden tables and seats. We had just found a good seat when two boys our age came from the other side and sat down opposite us. Somehow I knew: before long we would get to know these two strangers. The only question was: how would Melissa do it this time?

I didn't have to wait long. Suddenly, Melissa reached down and took something out of one of her shopping bags. It was a pink t-shirt. On the front of it was written, "Wanted Dead or Alive: Boys!" She showed it to me in such a way that the boys could see it, too. "What do you think?" she asked me. "Do you like it?"

One of the boys started laughing, then the other.

"What are you guys laughing at?" Melissa said to them.

"Dead or alive?" said the bigger boy, emphasizing the word "dead". "What good is a *dead* boy?"

That's how it got started. We soon found out that the taller boy was called Seth and the shorter boy Clarence, that they were from Wood Island, which is about halfway between downtown Boston and Revere Beach, and that they were both in their second year of high school. They told us that they'd come to downtown Boston to get some stuff for their computers.

My first reaction was "Oh, no! Computer nerds", but I soon realized that they were anything but nerdy. They were very interested in us and asked all kinds of questions.

Then Clarence said that they were going to a public concert and asked if we wanted to go along. Melissa wanted to know who was playing – as if that made any difference – and before I knew it, I could hear her saying, "Oh, yeah. We're with you, aren't we, Dee?"

Although we had only just met Seth and Clarence, I was already asking myself how long the "flirt" would last this time. This thought, I noticed, was making it difficult for me to connect up with them. I tried to have a good time with them at the concert and afterwards at Dunkin Donuts, but I felt strange, like an actor playing a part.

Melissa asked me afterwards what was wrong. I told her I had a headache. She looked at me in a funny way and said that I shouldn't think so much.

Seth said they were going on a whale watch the next day and asked would we like to come with them? Before I could say anything, Melissa had already answered for us: Yes! she said.

## Chapter 6 Whale Watching

The next morning seemed to be the start of a beautiful day, but just as we were getting on the catamaran the wind picked up. Moments later, as the sea began to get rough, the captain of the catamaran advised the passengers to take motion pills. Luckily, Seth had brought some with him and we all took one. It was a good thing we did. After moving slowly out of the harbor, the catamaran suddenly started going through the five-foot waves at a heart-stopping speed.

I was doing deep-breathing exercises to keep my breakfast down. Seth laughed and asked me if I knew why we were going so fast. "The captain's training for the Olympics?" I asked with a straight face. That cracked Seth up.

"A good answer," he said. "But it's not gold medals he's after, it's money. This is a three-hour cruise. Which means that we have to be back in the harbor in three hours – for the next group of paying customers."

"Right," I said. "And the busy time for tourists is basically only in the summer months, so they have to make the best of it."

"Yeah, get out to the whales and get back fast, no matter how rough the waters are."

For once, Melissa wasn't saying much. She was just sitting there trying not to get sick.

Clarence was in the restroom. When he returned he looked unhappy. "Lots of sick people there," he said. "I had to wait ten minutes to get inside. Bad scene."

An hour later the catamaran slowed down. The passengers, many of them with white faces, got up and went outside. Seth took me by the hand and led me outside, too. Clarence and Melissa followed us.

"Oh, look!" I cried. "There they are. A whole bunch of whales!"

"Where, where?" cried Melissa. I pointed toward the front of the catamaran. There, in the distance, were shiny dark shapes rolling around in the water.

The passengers pushed forward, everyone wanting to get in a good position to see the whales. Seth and I were pressed together in the crowd. For the next half hour I not only enjoyed watching the whales, I also enjoyed standing very close to Seth and feeling his body next to mine. He seemed to enjoy it, too. He squeezed my hand and smiled at me.

The whales seemed to enjoy that half hour, too. Some of them were real crowd-pleasers. When the people applauded them, they did even more crowd-pleasing things like waving with their tails.

As we watched them, I began to realize that they weren't all alike, but that each one of them was different, with a personality of its own. They were a lot like humans in that way. Some of them came right up close to the boat, others stayed further away.

Two of them stayed close together, apparently good "friends". One of them was the champion jumper. When "Air Jordan", as Seth called him, came sailing up out of the water, a loud "Ooohhhhhhhh!" went through the crowd. Another was a real entertainer, always doing something to make people laugh. Like suddenly diving down and minutes later popping up beside the boat. One of the larger ones seemed to be having fun scaring people. It would come racing through the water straight for the boat only to turn away at the last second! Then there was the clever one,

which used the boat to help it catch fish by driving them toward the side of the catamaran so they couldn't get away.

The one I watched most was the injured one, a huge gray whale with a large piece missing from its tail. I felt sorry for it and wondered what had happened. Did it get hit by a ship? Was it attacked by sharks? Did it get caught in a net? In the end, when I realized that it could swim almost as well as the others, I stopped feeling sorry for it.

There was great excitement on the boat on the way back. Everyone was talking at the same time. Most of them had forgotten all about the rough trip to get to the whales and how sick they had become. It was worth it, they said. It was more than worth it, one of them said. It was an unforgettable experience. The others all nodded.

Seth stayed very close to me during the trip back, although the crowd wasn't pressing us together now. He didn't say much. Maybe he was thinking about the whales – or maybe he was thinking about what I was thinking about …

## **Chapter 7** Two Tourists from Germany

We were together with Seth and Clarence three more times and then came what I knew and feared would come: Melissa decided it was time for a change – again! This time I protested. I said that I didn't like the game she was playing. "What do you call your game?" I asked her. "Rent-a-Boy?" She didn't like that and said that maybe I'd like to try my luck alone in Boston. She didn't call on me for the next two days.

By the time she came around on the third day I was happy to see her again. She acted as if nothing had happened and asked me if I was interested in the history of Boston. Yes, of course, I said. Would I like to take a guided tour along the famous Freedom Trail with her? Oh yes, I would, I said. Secretly, I asked myself if this was perhaps Melissa's way of showing me that she wasn't only interested in boys.

The tour started at Boston Common. We joined a small group of about ten tourists. Our guide was a gray-haired man with thick glasses who was so full of information that he could have gone on talking about any of the 16 sites for hours. Thankfully, he only had two hours for the tour so he had to keep going.

From Boston Common we went to the New State House, then on to Park Street Church, then to the Granary Burying Ground and finally to King's Chapel, where we were given a ten-minute break. My head was aching from the hot sun and from all the facts the guide thought we should know. Melissa smiled at me sweetly and asked how I was enjoying the tour. I smiled back and wondered if this was her way of punishing me for what I had said to her about her "game".

After the too-short break, the guide pushed on to the Ben Franklin Statue, then to the Old Corner Bookstore and the Old South Meeting House. As the sun grew hotter, I kept glancing over at Melissa. I hoped that she would notice that I was tired – and bored, but she only smiled her sweet smile. Now I was almost sure that this was her way of getting back at me.

But when we reached the Paul Revere House an hour later and she noticed two boys looking our way, she turned to me and laughed. A moment later, after she had managed to get into a conversation with the boys, she signaled to me to join them.

I almost laughed out loud. The guided-tour Melissa had changed back into her true self.

The boys, tourists from Germany, were really good looking, both of them. Dirk was the taller – the one for me. Sven, the elegantly-dressed one, was just right for Melissa.

I was very surprised at how well they could speak English. Dirk told me that they had been learning English ever since the third grade. Melissa laughed and said that she and I would have to be careful with our English when talking to them. Sven didn't realize that she was joking and said that we should talk normally because they preferred "real" English to the classroom version of English they had learned. I smiled and said I thought their English was just fine.

Dirk was a real gentleman. I could see that he had a problem. He was obviously trying to think of a way to get us away from the tour group, but was too polite to say it. Melissa helped him. She said that the tour guide was boring and she could use a break. Delighted, Dirk asked us if we'd like to join them for a cappuccino. That was the end of our history lesson and the beginning of our "German lesson".

The two of them laughed a lot while we were drinking our cappuccinos. I asked myself why. Was it because they were nervous? Or do all German boys laugh a lot?

They said they were students in a *Gymnasium* (the way Sven said it sounded like "Gim-nah-zee-um"), a kind of high school, and that in two more years they would, as he said, get their *Abitur* ("Ah-be-tuuah"). As I understood it, this was something like our high school diploma.

They said they were staying at the youth hostel in Kenmore, right across from Fenway Park, the Red Sox baseball stadium. That information was, of course, music to Melissa's ears, and she immediately began to talk about baseball and her favorite team, the Red Sox. Noticing how interested they were, she asked if they had ever been to a Red Sox game. No, they hadn't, but they would like to, they both said at once. At that point, Melissa smiled and said no problem, we could go tomorrow, she could get us tickets. The boys grinned with excitement. Melissa gave me a knowing look and I grinned, too.

## Chapter 8 At the Ball Park

Watching a major league baseball game was a new experience not only for Dirk and Sven. I had never been to one, either! Melissa was an expert. She often went to games with her father, so she knew everything about the practical things like where to buy the tickets, where the best seats were, where to find the toilets, etc.

Not only that, she also knew all about the rules. As soon as we got to our seats, she asked the boys if they wanted a "quick" explanation of the basic rules of baseball. Of course they did.

She began by pointing at the playing field. "A baseball field is called a diamond," she said, "because the inner part, the infield, is shaped like a diamond. Do you see it? Can you see the diamond?"

"Sure," both of them said.

"Okay. You see those three bags? Well, they are called bases and they are the corners of the diamond: first base on the right, second base in the middle and third base on the left. The fourth corner is that white plate, called home plate. In the middle of the diamond is the mound – do you see it? It's a little higher than the rest of the infield. It's where the pitcher throws from."

"I see it," said Sven and Dirk said, "Me, too."

Melissa pointed at the field again. "Do you see the outer part – the part between the infield and the fence?"

Both boys only nodded. What they were really looking at – staring at pop-eyed – was a man coming up the stairs towards them. He was carrying what looked like a big box hanging from his neck and crying, "Hot dogs! Get your hot dogs here!" Every now and then he would stop, put down his box, pull out a hot dog, put it in a bun and add whatever the customer wanted to it.

When Melissa noticed that the boys had stopped listening to her, she smiled at me. "Right," she said. "That's part of the game, too: hot dogs! An important part. Let's have some hot dogs. We'll be here for the next three hours and we don't want to be hungry, do we? Come on, it's on me."

The boys grinned like two little kids.

"Four over here," Melissa said and the vendor came to us and put down his box. A moment later, all of us were holding a steaming hot dog. The boys' grins had grown even wider. They were about to take their first bite when Melissa suddenly put up her hand.

"Stop!" she said. "You can't eat a hot dog without a Coke."

I noticed that the boys weren't too happy about having to wait, but they were too polite to protest. Dirk jumped up. "Okay. Where do I go to get them?"

"Nowhere," said Melissa. "They're coming to you. Look!" She pointed down the stairs where a vendor was coming our way crying, "Ice cold Coke! Ice cold Coke!" A few moments later he reached us. Melissa offered to buy the drinks, but the boys paid, saying it was their turn this time.

Now, finally, the boys were ready and took their first bite of a real American hot dog. I waited a moment, watching them closely. "Well?" I said.

Dirk gave a little smile and pointed at his mouth, which was very full. Sven had the same problem and made a just-a-moment signal with his hand. Both of them were chewing quickly. That cracked Melissa up. I started laughing, too.

Moments later, his mouth still full, Dirk said, "Mm ... very good!"

"Very, very good!" Sven said, his mouth just as full, and we all laughed.

When the laughter had calmed down, Melissa gave the two a serious look. "Okay, so maybe now we can get back to the basics of baseball. I was talking about the outer part of the diamond, the part between the infield and the fence. I'd like to go on now, if that's okay with you."

The boys looked up from their hot dogs for a moment and nodded. "Go ahead, Melissa," Dirk said, but he looked more interested in his hot dog.

"Well, that part is called the outfield and it's divided into right field, center field and left field. There are nine players on each team and each of them has a position. There are three players in the outfield, one for each part of the field. And there are four in the infield, one at each base and one between second and third base. Finally, there's the pitcher and the one who catches the balls the pitcher throws, the catcher. His position is behind the plate. Any questions?"

"The guy behind the catcher is the referee, right?" Sven asked.

"Right, except in baseball he's called the umpire."

Suddenly, Dirk noticed that I was looking at him with a big grin on my face. "What's so funny, Dee?"

"It's your moustache," I said.

"Moustache? I don't have a moustache."

"You do now. A yellow one – a mustard moustache!"

Sven looked at him and gave out a loud laugh.

"What are you laughing about?" Dirk said. "You've got one yourself."

"Oh."

"Here," said Melissa. "I took these just in case." She gave each of them two or three paper napkins. The boys rubbed their faces and looked at each other. Then they rubbed some more.

Meanwhile, people had been pouring into the stadium, filling the seats around us. Suddenly, there was a great roar as the Red Sox came out onto the field.

"Let me try to finish explaining the game to you before it's too late," Melissa said, almost shouting to make herself heard. "Baseball is quite complicated, but basically it's like soccer and most other sports: the aim of the game is to score more points than the other team. A team scores points when their players get all the way around the bases to home plate. The main way to get on base is by hitting the ball. The team in the field must try to stop the other team from scoring points. There are many ways they can do this. One way is by catching a ball that's hit into the air before it comes down. Another way is by catching a ball that's hit on the ground and throwing it to first base before the player who hit it gets there. Of course, another way is for the pitcher to throw three good balls that the batter doesn't hit. That's called a strikeout. If you – "

Just then someone started singing the national anthem and we all had to stand up.

After that, there was another great roar from the crowd and the game started. "If you have any questions during the game – anything you don't understand – please ask," Melissa said.

The boys nodded, happy that the explanation was over.

It was a good day for the Red Sox. They won the game 6–3.

The crowd was buzzing with excitement as they left the stadium. Boston fans love the Red Sox, especially when they win. Dirk and Sven had really enjoyed the game and thanked Melissa for the tickets. They asked us if we'd like to see their room at the hostel. I was about to say yes but Melissa suggested that we go somewhere and get something to eat instead. So we went to a nearby Burger King.

Dirk and Sven were still excited about the game and continued talking about it while we ate. The highlight of the game for Dirk was the home run. Melissa said that it was a really long home run, one of the longest she'd ever seen. "No wonder," she said, her eyes shining, "It was Manny Rodriguez who hit it. He's known for his record-breaking home runs." You could see that Melissa thought a lot of Manny.

After we'd talked about the game a long time, Sven asked us if we liked soccer. He and Dirk both played on the same team, he said. This was my chance to say something. I play soccer, too. In fact, I'm on our high school team. Dirk wanted to know how popular soccer was in the U.S. I told him it wasn't as popular as the big three American sports, football, baseball and basketball, but that it was growing in popularity, partly because it was the favorite sport of the Latinos, the Latin American immigrants.

Dirk looked at me, shook his head and said he couldn't understand why Americans didn't like soccer as much as Germans and the rest of the world. I didn't know the answer, but said that maybe it's because Americans like action and find it boring to watch a long game in which very few or no goals are scored. Maybe they prefer sports like football or basketball because there are a lot more "goals". Also, at school, football and soccer are both played in the fall. You have to choose between them – you can't play both – and most students choose to play football.

Melissa ended our discussion about soccer by saying that we had to catch the subway and get back. I was disappointed and couldn't understand why she was in such a hurry to return home, and I almost said something. Almost.

Dirk said that they were flying back to Germany in two days and asked if we could do something together on their last day. After a short discussion, Melissa decided that the best idea was a day at the beach. She said we'd meet them at the Downtown Crossing subway station at noon.

## Chapter 9 Meet-and-run?

It was already almost 11 o'clock and I was getting uneasy. I hadn't heard from Melissa since we got home last night. If we were going to meet Dirk and Sven at twelve she would have to be here soon. The last thing she said last night was that she'd drop by early enough to get to the subway in plenty of time. Okay, it takes fifteen to twenty minutes for the subway to get from Stony Brook to Downtown Crossing, I said to myself. So what am I worrying about?

Ten minutes later I decided to go over to Melissa's and check on her. I would act as if nothing was wrong. I didn't want to make her think I didn't trust her.

When her mother came to the door, she was surprised to see me and said that Melissa hadn't said anything about meeting me this morning. She asked me to wait a moment while she went upstairs.

A few minutes later she returned and told me that Melissa was still in bed and didn't want to get up yet. Somehow I had expected that. I got angry and told her that I had to talk with Melissa. She was about to say something, but I ran past her before she could open her mouth. I hurried up the stairs. I gave a short sharp knock on the door to Melissa's bedroom and went inside without waiting for an answer.

Melissa was lying somewhere under the bed covers. "Melissa!" I said loudly. "Wake up. It's 11.20!"

There was a movement in the bed and then a head appeared. Melissa slowly opened her eyes and looked at me. "Dee? What are you doing here?" she said.

"We promised to meet Dirk and Sven at 12 o'clock, remember?" I said trying not to shout.

"Oh, Dee, you always take these things so seriously," she said. "Listen. We've had a nice time with Dirk and Sven. That doesn't mean we have to make a habit of them."

"HABIT?" I cried. "WE JUST MET THEM THREE DAYS AGO! How can you talk about a habit! You're playing your game again, only this time it's not Boy-For-A-Week, it's Boy-For-Three-Days. Where do we go from here? The next time it'll be Boy-For-A-Day and then – AND THEN – WHAT COMES AFTER THAT?"

Melissa sat up in bed, wide awake now, and gave me a long hard look. "And what's your game? Boy-For-Life? Aren't you a little young for that? Listen, Dee, I don't want to sound like your mother but take a little advice from me: you're only young once. It's the time to have fun and get to meet a lot of boys. Which might be useful later, if you decide to choose a partner. It can help you know what kind of partner you want."

I fought back my anger and forced myself to smile. "You're right. It is important to meet lots of different boys when you're young," I began slowly. "But I have a problem with what you mean by the word 'meet'. To me, meeting someone means getting to know them, which means spending time with them. We've been with Dirk and Sven twice now. Is that enough time to get to know them?" I paused to give my words effect. When I spoke again, my voice was full of irony. "But maybe I'm different than you. Maybe country girls like me are slower than city girls like you."

Melissa let out a nervous little laugh. "Yeah, maybe we are," is all she said.

"Come on, Melissa! You know that it hasn't got anything to do with city or town." I stepped up closer to the bed. "I think you've got a problem with boys. You want to be with boys, but at the same time you want to keep them at a distance. You don't want to let them get too close to you."

Melissa narrowed her eyes. "Well, well, Little Miss Psychologist," she said slowly. "You think you see right through me, don't you?"

"Enough to know that you've got a problem."

My answer surprised her. She'd assumed that I would back off. Now she hesitated. "What kind of a problem do you think it is, Miss Psychologist?" Her tone was less sarcastic this time.

I looked her straight in the eye. "My guess is that a boy hurt you. Am I right? Did you get hurt?"

For what seemed to be a full minute, Melissa just sat therc, staring at me.

"Melissa?"

Suddenly, she dived down and pulled the covers up over her face. I didn't know what was going on at first, but then I saw the covers were shaking. I realized that she was crying.

I wanted to reach out and touch her but made myself hold back. After a while, the covers stopped shaking and she looked out. Her eyes were wet and red.

For a long moment she fixed those eyes on me, studying my face. I felt like my face was burning and wanted to turn away, but forced myself to hold her gaze. At last, she said, "You're right, Dee. I got hurt – real bad." She started crying again.

I waited a moment and then said, "Tell me about it – if you want to."

Melissa got out a Kleenex and dried her eyes. She took a deep breath. "It was last year in school. His name was Scott. We – we went together for about two months. I thought it would last forever. The first weeks with him were heaven, but then he started putting me under pressure. He kept saying things like I was holding back on him, being unfair to him. He said it was time for me to show my feelings and prove to him that I was his girl. I told him that I wasn't ready. I said it was too soon. But he only got angry and said he wasn't going to wait much longer. And he didn't. In the end, he dropped me. I'll never forget what he said the last time we were together. He said I was cold and guys don't go for cold girls. I would never have another boyfriend, he said." Melissa looked at me with a sad little smile.

I took her hand and pressed it tight. “You’re lucky to be rid of a guy like that,” I said. “He only wanted to use you.”

“I – I know. But it hurt. And it still hurts – being dropped like that – like a sack of garbage.”

“He’s the sack of garbage, not you! You shouldn’t feel bad about what happened. He’s the one who should feel bad.” I paused, looking for the right words for what I wanted to say. “Scott was a scumbag and he hurt you, but you’ve got to put that behind you and get on with your life. You’ve got to realize that most boys are not like that. You’ve got to give them a chance.”

“I – I can’t. I’m too afraid – afraid to get hurt again.”

“Nobody wants to get hurt. I can understand that. But meet-and-run is not the answer. You’ve got to learn how to trust again, that’s what you’ve got to do. You’ve got to forget about Scott and give other boys a fair chance.” I smiled warmly.

“Will you help me?” she said.

“Of course I will.” I ran my fingers slowly through her hair.

She looked up at me, uncertain, her red eyes running up and down my face. For what seemed like several minutes, she continued to look at me in silence. Finally, she gave me a weak smile and said, “Okay. Give me a few minutes to get ready. I’ll hurry. We don’t want to keep our German friends waiting, do we?”

## Chapter 10 The Wave Hunters

It was shortly after twelve o'clock when our train reached Downtown Crossing. Sven and Dirk were waiting for us. We caught the next train heading for State and changed there to the Blue Line. Ten minutes later, we got out at Revere Beach and hurried down to the promenade. The two boys looked up and down the beach, amazed at the panoramic view. It was a beautiful sunny day with not a cloud in the sky. There were already crowds of people, not unusual for a Saturday.

As soon as we had found a nice spot near the water, Dirk and Sven wanted to go for a swim. Melissa said she'd rather get some sun first, so she and I sat and watched as the two boys waded into the water.

"I'm impressed," Melissa said.

"With what?"

"With our two friends from Germany. I thought they were a little on the skinny side, but hey look at those bods!" Melissa gave a long, low whistle.

I laughed. I like boys with muscles, too, and had already noticed that Dirk and Sven were in really good shape. "Not only that, they're also good swimmers," I said, watching them cut through the water.

"I'm glad I came," Melissa said quickly.

"We'll have a good, good time," I said.

"If you want to go in swimming, go ahead. I'll be right here watching you."

"I think I will. Sure you don't want to come?" I said.

"No, go ahead. Maybe I'll join you a little later. It always takes me a while to go from warm beach to cold water. When it gets too hot here in the sun I'll join you."

I didn't want to wait. I hurried across the beach and waded in. Dirk and Sven were quite far out and didn't notice me at first. When I got closer to them, I shouted and they swam over to me.

"Where's Melissa?" Sven asked.

"Right where we left her. It takes her a while to get in the cold water. She likes to get nice and warm before she's ready to swim."

"I like to do it the other way around," Sven said. "Swim first and then warm up on the beach." He seemed a little disappointed.

I was enjoying myself too much to worry about Melissa. Dirk was making big eyes at me in my bikini. "It's okay," I said to Sven. "She'll join us in a little while."

I saw a big wave coming and jumped into it. The boys did the same and we were all carried along, up and down, like surfers without surfboards, towards shore. When we reached the beach Melissa was standing there waiting for us. Sven was delighted. He took her by the hand and led her out into the water.

"Okay, guys," he said, laughing. "Follow me. We're wave-hunters. We're looking for the biggest and wildest waves this ocean's got. Come on!"

"Yeah, bring them on!" Dirk shouted.

Dirk and I followed Sven and Melissa and we waded out until we were all almost up to our necks in water. Laughing with excitement, we stood there watching and waiting. We didn't have to wait long. A huge wave soon appeared. I don't know about the others, I was a little frightened by the size of it. But our laughter became wilder and wilder as it came nearer. When it hit us, I closed my eyes and let myself go with the flow, as they say. I felt like a feather in the wind.

When I opened my eyes again, the others were all around me and we all started laughing again.

Many monster waves later, we were ready for a rest. For the next half hour or so we all lay side by side in the sand, not saying much. Suddenly, Dirk sat up. “Hey,” he said. “A soccer game!”

Down the beach, on the other side of the lifeguard’s tower, several boys – they looked like Latinos – were playing beach soccer. Sven and I sat up immediately.

“Wow,” Sven said and gave a short whistle. “They’re good.”

“Really good,” Dirk said. “I wonder if they’d let us play.”

“Maybe you, but not me. They wouldn’t let a girl play,” I said.

“Come on, Dee,” Dirk said. “We’ll ask them.”

Surprise, surprise, they let me play. I played on the same team with Dirk and Sven along with three of the others. It was a fantastic game. I couldn’t believe how well Dirk and Sven played but the Latino boys were good, too, small but very quick. Beach soccer is a difficult game. You want to run fast and make your moves but the sand holds you back. You have to work twice as hard as on grass. I was out of breath after five minutes but I hung on. The game went on and on until finally, someone shouted, “Next goal wins!”

That was Dirk’s finest hour. He did a double pass with me and got free. At the last moment, he kicked the ball over to Sven, who had an easy shot and made the goal.

We thanked the boys for letting us play. I could see that they really admired Dirk and Sven. They were looking at me differently now, too.

Melissa came over. She gave us each a happy fist bump. “You guys were really great,” she said. Then, to me: “I don’t know how you do it, Dee. You were just as good as the boys – except for Dirk and Sven, of course." She winked and laughed. "It's time," she said, "for the Revere Beach soccer champs to receive their prize. I'm taking orders. What will it be? An ice cream cone? A milkshake? Just tell me what you want and I'll get it."

I ordered my usual, a coffee milkshake. The boys asked for the same. We felt great about winning the game. It also felt good to rest while someone went and got milkshakes for you.

A little later, when Melissa returned, we heard loud music coming from down the beach. I turned and saw a large crowd. "What's going on down there?" I said.

"It's a karaoke contest," Melissa said. "I saw the sign at the ice cream place. WERS Boston is putting it on."

"Why don't we go and check it out? Maybe we can win a prize," I said. "How about it, guys? Are you interested?"

"I don't know," Dirk said.

"Oh, come on." Sven laughed and gave him a little push.

"Well, okay, but I'll just watch," Dirk said. "I can't sing."

## Chapter 11 A Hard Test

"Did Dirk really sing?" Melissa asked me. We were on our way home after our wonderful day at Revere Beach. We'd just said goodbye to the boys at Downtown Crossing station and were waiting for an Orange Line train to Forest Hills.

"I'm not sure. I couldn't really hear him. He was moving his lips but maybe he was only faking it. Anyway, no one seemed to notice," I said. "Sven sang loud enough for both of them."

"Loud and good. I still think we should have got a prize."

I looked closely at Melissa. "Their plane leaves tomorrow at 11.30, they said."

"Yeah, I know." Melissa closed her eyes a moment. "That'll be hard for me."

"What do you mean?"

"Don't you understand? I – I like Sven. I –" Melissa couldn't go on.

"Hey, come on." I rested my hand on Melissa's back. "I like Dirk, too. And it'll be hard for me to see him leave tomorrow, too. But we'll stay in touch. I'm sure we will."

"I wish I could be as cool about it as you."

"You've got to work at it, Melissa. Saying goodbye has a lot to do with trust, you know. Just keep trusting Sven."

"Saying goodbye has to do with trust? Now what does that mean?"

I took Melissa by the hand. "It simply means that you accept the fact that he is leaving. You let him go. You don't try to hang onto him. And, most importantly, you believe that you'll see him again, some time, some place."

Just then our train came and we got in. It was only half full so we found a seat by ourselves quickly. Melissa turned away and looked out the window. I could see that she was thinking hard.

Finally, she turned to me and said, "What you were talking about before – about saying goodbye – I understand up here" – she pointed at her head – "but in here – " she put her hand on her heart, "there's something else going on. When Scott dropped me it did something to me – in here." There was a please-try-to-understand-me look in Melissa's eyes.

"I know, I know," I said softly, putting my arm around her shoulder. "You trusted him and he misused your trust. That hurt! But you've got to learn to trust again. It's the only way. You're on the right track. You're doing just fine. But now your trust is facing a hard test: Sven is leaving." I looked Melissa deep in the eye. "Don't get that mixed up with Scott leaving you. Sven is not Scott. You can trust Sven, believe me."

For several moments, Melissa was quiet. I thought it best to be quiet, too, and let her be alone with her thoughts. After a while, she put her hand on mine and gave me a little smile. "Thanks, Dee. You've helped me understand my situation much better. Now I know what I *should* do," she said, emphasizing the word 'should'. She lowered her eyes. "Still, it's not easy for me ..."

We didn't say much after that. Melissa was looking out the window again. I knew what was going on. Head and heart, two voices within her trying to be heard. Which would she listen to? I had said all I could say. Now it was up to Melissa.

## Chapter 12 Last-minute Goodbyes

The next morning Melissa came to get me. Together we walked to Stony Brook Station. We were talking loudly and laughing a lot. At the station, people stared at us. Luckily, we didn't have to wait long for the Oak Grove train.

Ten minutes later, we reached State, where we had to change trains to get to the airport. As we waited at the station I looked at my watch. 9.45. Another ten or fifteen minutes at the latest, I thought. I had told Dirk we'd be there around 10 o'clock. That would give us an hour with them before boarding time.

When our train, the Blue Line for Wonderland, came along a few minutes later, Melissa and I got on quickly. The train was full and we had to stand. A moment later we were on our way. I could feel myself growing nervous. I was thinking of Dirk and about what I would say to him and wondering – what would he say to me?

Suddenly, the train came to a stop. Everyone looked around. What was going on? Then the driver's voice came over the loudspeaker. "There's been an accident at Maverick. There will be a delay of about ten minutes."

Melissa looked at me and shook her head. "The good old Boston subway. Always good for a surprise."

"Ten minutes – we'll still have lots of time to see the guys off."

"Yeah, *if* it's only ten minutes." Melissa stressed the word 'if'. "The problem is, they always say 'ten minutes'. The last time I was in a subway and they said 'ten minutes', we had to wait half an hour!" Melissa gave a short, sarcastic laugh.

Fifteen minutes later, the driver's voice came over the loudspeaker again. "I've just been informed that we'll have to wait a little longer. Please remain calm. We'll be moving again as soon as possible."

The passengers sat very still. Some of them were reading, some were talking quietly, others just sat there. This situation wasn't new. They knew that there was nothing they could do about it – but wait.

I knew that, too, but I couldn't sit still. Melissa looked at me helplessly. Minutes that seemed like hours were going by. Minutes we could – should be spending with Dirk and Sven. I looked at my watch again. 10.30. Oh, please, dear God, I prayed, let us get moving again.

God didn't seem to be interested in my prayer. We waited some more. I tried to be optimistic. "We'll still have time to say goodbye if we get there soon," I said.

"It'll have to be very soon. Even if they wait for us they'll have to board within the next half hour. Most … "

Just then the train started moving again. I counted the minutes to Airport Station. As soon as the train arrived we got out and ran to the shuttle bus. Fortunately, we were just on time. Unfortunately, the bus stopped at each terminal and ours was the last one, E, for international flights. When we finally got there, we ran into the terminal and hurried to the gate Dirk said they'd be at. The big clock on the wall said 10.49!

Near the gate, we could see a long line of people and – there, almost at the end of the line – stood Dirk and Sven! When we reached them, we were so out of breath we couldn't say a word at first. Without saying anything, the two boys took us in their arms. Half crying, I told them why we were so late.

"It's not your fault. There's nothing you could do about it," Dirk said.

"We're glad you got here. Don't worry about it," Sven added.

The line, I noticed, was moving quickly and the boarding gate was getting nearer. "Will you be coming back to Boston next year?" I asked.

Dirk looked at Sven. Both nodded. "We'd like to. It's hard to say. But what about you and Melissa? Why don't you come to Germany?" Dirk said.

Taken by surprise, I looked at Melissa. She was smiling. "We'd – we'd love to," she said.

"Well, you've got our email addresses. We'll stay in touch, won't we?"

"Oh, yes!" Melissa and I said at the same time.

"We could help you plan your trip. Maybe you could come during the Christmas vacation. Flights are cheap in the winter. We could pick you up at the airport."

Suddenly, just before he reached the gate, Dirk took me in his arms again and we kissed. When I opened my eyes, I saw that Sven and Melissa were doing the same.

Then I noticed that the ticket man was smiling at us. "I hate to interrupt, but can I have your boarding cards please."

The boys went through the gate but turned and waved to us before they were out of sight. My eyes zoomed in on Dirk's face. Our eyes met and a strong, warm feeling flashed through me.

When I turned to Melissa she had a smile on her face. "Hey," I said with mock seriousness, "what are you so happy about? I thought you'd be sad now that Sven has gone."

TERMINAL E
10:49
TERMINAL E
10:49

"You heard what they said. They want us to come and visit them!"

"Yeah, wouldn't that be great?"

"I'm so happy that I was here to say goodbye to him," Melissa said thoughtfully.

"You almost didn't make it," I said, looking her in the eye.

Melissa nodded slowly, then gave me a knowing smile. "You're right. In more ways than one. But, thanks to you, Dee, I did make it." There were tears in Melissa's eyes as she took me in her arms. She held me tight for a long time. Then, hand in hand, we left the terminal.

## Questions and Activities

### Chapter 1

1 Find Dee's hometown, Hartsville, on a map of the USA. How do you think it is different to Boston?

2 In pairs or small groups, discuss Dee's opinion about small-town boys. Do you think she is right?

### Chapter 2

1 What does Billy tell the girls about himself and his family?

2 Use the Internet to find out more about Revere Beach and add to the information given about it in chapter 2.

### Chapter 3

1 How did Dee react when Melissa decided it was time to stop meeting Billy and Miles? How does her reaction compare to Melissa's?

2 Why do you think Melissa doesn't want to meet up with the two boys? Discuss your ideas with the class.

### Chapter 4

1 What "methods" did Melissa use to get to know Ben and Michael?

2 Use the Internet to find out more about the Boston Red Sox. Make a list of interesting facts about the present team or past teams.

## Chapter 5

1 Why did Dee feel strange when she met the two new boys, Seth and Clarence?

2 In groups of four, make up a dialogue that Seth, Clarence, Melissa and Dee might have had at Dunkin Donuts after the concert.

## Chapter 6

1 Make a list of the different kinds of whales Dee and Seth watched.

2 In pairs, choose one of the whales described in the chapter and find out more information about it. Make notes and/or drawings for a class presention.

## Chapter 7

1 Explain what was different about Dee's reaction this time when Melissa said it was time for a change again.

2 In pairs, change the indirect speech of the last three paragraphs of the chapter (starting with "They said they were students …") to direct speech. Begin like this: "We are students in a '*Gymnasium*'," Dirk said. "In two more years we will …"

## Chapter 8

1 In pairs, use the information Melissa gives to draw a picture of a baseball diamond. Try to include the nine players in their respective positions.

2 Use the Internet to find out more about soccer in the USA. Has it become more popular since David Beckham started to play in America?

## Chapter 9

1 Explain in your own words what Scott did that hurt Melissa.
2 Do you think Melissa's reaction is understandable? Discuss your opinion with the class.

## Chapter 10

1 Explain what Sven meant by "wave-hunters".
2 In pairs, make up three sentences about the contents of the chapter, two of them true and one false. Ask another pair of students to decide which sentences are true and which one is false.

## Chapter 11

1 At the end of the chapter Dee says about Melissa that there are "two voices within her trying to be heard". In pairs, work out at least three sentences coming from her heart.
2 In pairs, work out at least three sentences coming from Melissa's head.

## Chapter 12

1 When Dee says "You almost didn't make it," Melissa replies: "You're right. In more ways than one." What do you think she means?
2 Do you think Melissa and Dee will visit Germany?

## Extra Activity

Choose to be Melissa or Dee. Write an email to Sven or Dirk a week after they left Boston.

# Vocabulary

**A**

**algae** ['ældʒiː] Algen
**amusement park** [ə'mjuːzmənt pɑːk] Vergnügungspark, Rummelplatz
**apparently** [ə'pærəntli] anscheinend
(to) **applaud** [ə'plɔːd] Beifall klatschen
(to) **assume** [ə'sjuːm] vermuten
**awesome** ['ɔːsəm] fantastisch, großartig

**B**

**back and forth** ['bæk‿ənd fɔːθ] hin und her
**ballroom** ['bɔːlruːm] Festsaal, Tanzsaal
**base** [beɪs] *Spielstation beim Baseball*
**basics** ['beɪsɪks] das Grundsätzliche
**batter** ['bætə] Schläger
(to) **be alike** [ə'laɪk] einander ähneln
(to) **be into sth.** [bi] (*infml*) aktives Interesse an etwas haben/zeigen
**beach potato** ['biːtʃ pə'teɪtəʊ] *vgl:* couch potato; jmd. der am Strand faulenzt
**beachfront** ['biːtʒfrʌnt] am Strand
**beside** [bɪ'saɪd] neben
**bod (= body)** [bɒd] Körper
**boutique** [buː'tiːk] Boutique
**bowling alley** ['æli̥ 'bəʊlɪŋ‿ˌæli] Kegelbahn
**bumpy** ['bʌmpi] holprig
**bunch** [bʌntʃ] Gruppe
(to) **buzz with sth. (excitement)** [bʌz] von etwas schwirren
**by ourselves** [ɑː'selvz] *hier:* für uns allein

**C**

**catamaran** ['kætəmə'ræn] Katamaran
**catcher** ['kætʃə] Fänger
**chapel** ['tʃæpl] Kapelle
(to) **check sth. out** ['tʃek aʊt] (*infml*) etwas anschauen
**Chinese** [ˌtʃaɪ'niːz] chinesisch
**clam chowder** [klæm 'tʃaʊdə] eine Art Muschelsuppe
**coffee-flavored** ['fleɪvəd] mit Kaffee-Geschmack
**complicated** ['kɒmplɪkeɪtɪd] kompliziert
**cone** [kəʊn] Eiswaffel
(to) **crack sb. up** [kræk] jdn. zum Lachen bringen
**crowd-pleaser** [kraʊd 'pliːzə] (*infml*) Person (*hier:* der Wal), die einem Publikum gefällt
**cute** [kjuːt] niedlich, hübsch

## D

**deep-breathing exercises** ['bri:ðɪŋ] Atemübungen
**delay** [dɪ'leɪ] Verzögerung
**diploma** [dɪ'pləʊmə] Abschlusszeugnis
(to) **dive** [daɪv] (hinab)tauchen
**dude** [du:d] Kerl, Typ

## E

**eatery** ['i:təri] (*AE*) Restaurant, Esslokal
**elegantly-dressed** ['elɪgəntli‿drest] schick bekleidet
**excitement** [ɪk'saɪtmənt] Aufregung

## F

(to) **fake** [feɪk] *hier:* tun als ob
(to) **fear** [fɪə] Angst haben
**fist bump** [fɪst] *Freundliche Begrüßung, bei der Fäuste leicht aufeinander treffen*
(to) **fix your eyes on sth.** [fɪks] den Blick auf etwas richten
**forever** [fər'evə] für immer

## G

**gaze** [geɪz] Blick
(to) **glance at sth.** [glɑ:ns] einen Blick auf etwas werfen
**glorious** ['glɔ:riəs] herrlich, prächtig
**gray-haired** ['greɪ‿heə:d] grauhaarig
**Greek** [gri:k] griechisch
(to) **grin** [grɪn] grinsen
**grip** [grɪp] Griff
**guided-tour** ['gaɪdɪd tʊə] Führung

## H

**halfway** [ˌhɑ:f'weɪ] halbwegs, auf halbem Weg
**heart-stopping** ['hɑ:tstɒpɪŋ] atemberaubend, aufregend
(to) **hesitate** ['hezɪteɪt] zögern
**highlight** ['haɪlait] Höhepunkt
(to) **hurry over to sb.**['hʌri] auf jdn. zustürzen

## I

**immediately** [ɪ'mi:diətli] sofort
**infield** ['ɪnfi:ld] *quadratischen Teil des Spielfelds beim Baseball*
**irony** ['aɪrəni] Ironie

## J

**jellyfish** ['dʒelifɪʃ] Qualle

## K

**karaoke contest** [ˌkæri'əʊki‿'kɒntest] Karaoke-Wettbewerb
**Kleenex** ['kli:neks] eine Marke von Taschentüchern

## L

**lifeguard's tower** ['laɪfgɑ:dz 'taʊə] Rettungsturm
**line** [laɪn] (*AE*) Schlange
**lobster** ['lɒbstə] Hummer
(to) **loosen up** ['lu:sn] locker werden
(to) **lower** ['ləʊə] senken

## M

**major league baseball** [li:g] *Die Baseball Profiliga in den USA*

**meanwhile** ['mi:nwaɪl] mittlerweile

**medal** ['medl] Medaille

**Mexican** ['meksɪkən] mexikanisch

**mock seriousness** [mɒk 'sɪəriəsnəs] gespielter Ernst

**motion pills** ['məʊʃn pɪlʒ] Medikamente gegen Reisekrankheit

**mound** [maʊnd] *hier:* erhabene Abwurfstelle beim Baseball

**moustache** [mə'stɑ:ʃ] Schnurrbart

**mustard** ['mʌstəd] Senf

## N

**napkin** ['næpkɪn] Serviette

**navy** ['neɪvi] marine

**nearby** ['niə'baɪ] nahegelegen, in der Nähe

**nerd** [nɜ:d] (*infml*) Langweiler, Niete

## O

**only child** ['əʊnli; ˌəʊnli 'tʃaɪld] Einzelkind

**optimistic** [ˌɒptɪ'mɪstɪk] optimistisch

**outfield** ['aʊtfi:ld] *äußeren Teil des Spielfelds beim Baseball*

## P

**panoramic view** [ˌpænə'ræmɪk] Panoramablick

**pennant** ['penənt] Wimpel, Fahne (*das Siegeszeichen beim Baseball*)

**personality** [ˌpɜ:sə'næləti] Charakter

**pitcher** ['pɪtʃə] Werfer

(to) **pop out** [pɒp aʊt] *hier:* überrascht die Augen weit öffnen

(to) **pop up** [pɒp‿əp] *hier:* auftauchen

**pop-eyed** ['pɒpaid] (*infml*) mit weit geöffneten Augen

**popularity** [ˌpɒpju'lærəti] Popularität

(to) **pray** [preɪ] beten

**psychologist** [saɪ'kɒlədʒɪst] Psychologe

## R

(to) **rave about sth.** [reɪv] mit Begeisterung über etwas reden

**reconstruction work** [ˌri:kən'strʌkʃən wɜ:k] Wiederaufbau

**referee** [ˌrefə'ri:] Schiedsrichter

**rent-a-Boy** ['rentəbɔɪ] *vgl.* **rent-a-car:** *ein Junge zur Miete*

(to) **reopen** [ri'əʊpən] wiedereröffnen

(to) **rest sth. on** [rest] anliegen an etwas

**restroom** ['restru:m] (*AE*) Toilette

**roller coaster** ['rəʊlə‿ˌkəʊstə] Achterbahn

**roller skating rink** ['rəʊlə‿'skeɪtɪŋ rɪŋk] Rollschuhbahn

## S

**sack of garbage** ['gɑːbɪdʒ] Müllsack
(to) **scare** [skeə] erschrecken
**scumbag** ['skʌmbæg] Drecksack
**shark** [ʃɑːk] Hai
**shiny** ['ʃaɪni] glänzend
**skinny** ['skɪni] dünn, mager
**soccer** ['sɒkə] (*AE*) Fußball
**spot** [spɒt] Stelle
(to) **squeeze together** [skwiːz] zusammenquetschen/drängen
**steaming** ['stiːmɪŋ] dampfend
(to) **step up to sth.** [step] auf jdn./etwas zugehen
**strikeout** ['straɪkaʊt] Strikeout
**sudden** ['sʌdən] plötzlich
**surprise** [sə'praɪz] Überraschung

## T

**tail** [teɪl] Schwanz
**Thai** [tai] thailändisch
**thankfully** ['θæŋkfəli] zum Glück

## U

**umpire** ['ʌmpaɪə] Schiedsrichter
**uneasy** [ʌn'iːzi] nervös, ängstlich
**unfortunately** [ʌn'fɔːtʃənətli] leider

## V

**vendor** ['vendə] Verkäufer/in

## W

(to) **wade into** [weɪd] waten, *hier:* ins Wasser gehen
**WERS Boston** = *Lokaler Radiosender*
**whale** [weɪl] Wal
**wide awake** [waɪd‿ə'weɪk] hellwach
(to) **wink** [wɪŋk] zublinzeln

## Z

(to) **zoom in on sth.** [zuːm] etwas fokussieren

## Names

Air Jordan [eə 'dʒɔːdən]
Atlantic [ət'læntɪk]
Back Bay [bæk 'beɪ]
Ben Franklin [ben 'fræŋklɪn]
Billy ['bɪli]
Blue Line ['bluː laɪn]
Boston ['bɒstən]
Cambridge ['keɪmbridʒ]
Clarence ['klærəns]
Cyclone ['saɪkləʊn]
David Ortiz ['deɪvɪd 'ɔːrɪtz]
Deborah ['debrə]
Disneyland ['dɪznilænd]
Downtown Crossing
['daʊn'taʊn 'krɒsɪŋ]
Dunkin Donuts ['dʌŋkɪn 'dəʊnʌtz]
Faneuil ['fænjəl]
Fenway ['fenweɪ]
Filene [faɪ'lin]
Forest Hills ['fɒrɪst hɪlz]
Granary Burying Ground
['grænəri 'beriiŋ graʊnd]
Guy Lombardo [gaɪ lɒm'bɑːdeʊ]
Hartsville ['hɑːtsvɪl]
Harvard ['hɑːvəd]
Kelly ['keli]
Kenmore ['kenmɔː]
Macy ['meɪsi]
Manny Rodriguez
['mæni rɒ'driːgez]
Maverick ['mævərɪk]
Norah ['nɔːrə]
Oak Grove [əʊk greʊv]
Orange Line ['ɒrɪndʒ laɪn]
Orient Heights ['ɔːriənt haɪts]
Paul [pɔːl]
Red Sox [red sɒks]
Revere Beach [rɪ'vɪə biːtʃ]
Royal Canadians
['rɔɪəl kə'neɪdiənz]
Scott [skɒt]
Seth [seθ]
State [steɪt]
Stony Brook ['stəʊni brʊk]
Suffolk Downs ['sʌfək daʊnz]